Respect

Julie Murray

Abdo
CHARACTER EDUCATION
Kids

abdopublishing.com

Published by Abdo Kids, a division of ABDO, PO Box 398166, Minneapolis, Minnesota 55439.
Copyright © 2018 by Abdo Consulting Group, Inc. International copyrights reserved in all countries.
No part of this book may be reproduced in any form without written permission from the publisher.

Printed in the United States of America, North Mankato, Minnesota.

052017

092017

 THIS BOOK CONTAINS
RECYCLED MATERIALS

Photo Credits: Glow Images, iStock, Shutterstock

Production Contributors: Teddy Borth, Jennie Forsberg, Grace Hansen

Design Contributors: Christina Doffing, Candice Keimig, Dorothy Toth

Publisher's Cataloging in Publication Data

Names: Murray, Julie, 1969-, author.

Title: Respect / by Julie Murray.

Description: Minneapolis, Minnesota : Abdo Kids, 2018 | Series: Character
    education | Includes bibliographical references and index.

Identifiers: LCCN 2016962330 | ISBN 9781532100116 (lib. bdg.) |
    ISBN 9781532100802 (ebook) | ISBN 9781532101359 (Read-to-me ebook)

Subjects: LCSH: Respect--Juvenile literature. | Respect in children--Juvenile
    literature. | Children--Conduct of life--Juvenile literature. | Social skills in
    children--Juvenile literature.

Classification: DDC 179/.9--dc23

LC record available at http://lccn.loc.gov/2016962330

Table of Contents

Respect

Respect is all around.

Do you see it?

Cade helps Leo. He buckles his helmet. This is respect.

Tara uses good **manners**.

She says, "thank you."

Lou talks to his mom. He tells her the truth. He shows respect.

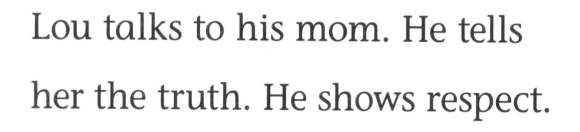

10

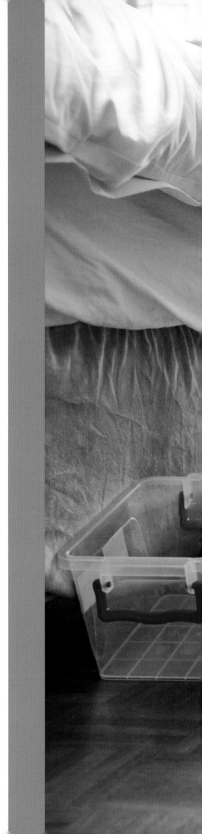

Manny made a mess!

He cleans it up.

Dan helps his mom.

He helps with **chores**.

Sara and Amy go fishing.

Amy waits her turn.

Ken listens to Ava.

It shows respect.

How do you show respect?

21

Some Ways to Be Respectful

Be Kind

Listen to Others

Take Turns

Use Good Manners

Glossary

chore
a common task around the house or yard.

manners
polite behavior.

Index

abdokids.com

Use this code to log on to abdokids.com and access crafts, games, videos, and more!

Abdo Kids Code:
CRK0116